D1066329

BLESSINGS IN
Freedom

DISPELLING THE MYTH

Kevin Boyd

ZYIA CONSULTING
Illuminate & Transcend

Blessings in Freedom: Dispelling the Myth

Copyright © 2021 by Kevin D Boyd

To contact the author, email kevboyd777@gmail.com.

ZYIA CONSULTING
Illuminate & Transcend

Zyia Consulting
Book Writing & Publishing Company
www.nyishaddavis.com
nyisha.d.davis@gmail.com
313.346.6189

Some names and identifying details have been changed within this book to protect the privacy of the individuals.

Unless otherwise noted, all Scripture quotations are taken from www.blueletterbible.org.

ISBN: 9798549419520

Printed in the United States of America.

Dedication

*Esther Cotton Harmon and Medina Lester, thank you
for your prayers and guidance to my freedom in Christ.
You helped me find God for myself. I pray the blessings of
the Lord will overtake you.*

Acknowledgment

Rest in peace, Ruthie Boyd, Mom. You introduced me to Christ. I'm forever grateful to have had you as long as I did.

Kimberly Bryant, you've been the sister I never had. Your obedience rescued me at a time where I felt completely hopeless.

Cynthia Moultrie, my dear longtime friend, God's kept us through all the ups and downs. We are blessed.

Heather Martin, my ace boon coon, shopping buddy, and personal chef, there's more for us.

Dawn Kingsby and my 'Boo Thang' Tonya King. You were there for me when nobody else was. God gave you to me, my Sunshine.

To all the many saints, ministers, friends, coworkers, and extended family that stood by me through my difficult times in life, I say thank you. You each know who you are. May God bless everyone.

Foreword

Julius Rhinehart

Life has shown and demonstrated to me that any and everybody can write a book. A trip to your average bookstore will reveal this. Just frequent your average bookstore and you will see a plethora of books dealing with a myriad of topics. In terms of accounts, testimonials, and autobiographies there a precious few are written by authors with the ability to pull you into the story. A few books are written by authors with the ability to not only pull you into the story but to make the story a teachable moment. What the reader is about to embark on, in the following account, is a story/testimony that not only pulls the reader into the story but also presents several teachable moments filled with practical life lessons. These lessons are not only helpful and insightful for those that are experiencing the same or a similar struggle as the author struggled with, but are also applicable for other areas.

The book that you hold in your hand, right now, is not something that came off of the top of the writer's head. Minister Kevin Boyd lived these pages. He has taken time to open up and share the wounds and scars of his past. He does this in a clear, concise, and transparent way. He does so not to boast or to magnify his past, but to take you through the various experiences that he went through in his life, pain, rejection, hurt, betrayal, salvation, redemption, and triumph to show and demonstrate through sharing the things that GOD did for him. It testifies that no matter what a person has been through, they don't have to be bound or defined by their past.

To sum this book up, I would use these words: Transparency and Instruction. This book serves as a testimony piece and a Deliverance Manuel all wrapped up into one. What I love about it is that it is di-

5

rect, non-compromising, transparent, and it isn't overly "preachy." This is a book that I would share and recommend sharing with someone that is in the lifestyle of homosexuality or is struggling with same-sex attraction. This is not something that the Church needs to compromise on but, it is also not something that we need to ignore. This is something that we need to deal with head on and do so in honesty, integrity, and love above all.

There are too many amongst us that are dealing with feelings, inclinations, and even double lives that need to be attended to and whose issues need to be addressed. These issues don't need to be addressed in a "bandaid" fashion. We need to go to the root of these issues and see to it by GOD'S Grace that our brothers and sisters gain deliverance. Minister Kevin Boyd does a masterful, as well an honest, job of helping get to root issues by sharing his issues well as what his triggers were. He also delves into something that I believe is of the utmost importance in dealing with these issues; identity.

I am proud of Minister Boyd. It takes courage to share these types of things with the world. To lay one's struggles bare for the world to see, scrutinize, takes being selfless in my view. I understand though that he is doing so for the sake of reaching those who are caught up in the same lifestyle he was caught up in or that are struggling with their identity. Above all, I am determined that he is doing his part in helping advance our Father's Kingdom. I am excited about this book. May the reader read it and digest its many insights and may they incorporate it in their lives as they live out our collective as assignment as Believers, as agents of reconciliation.

CONTENT

SPIRITUAL BONDAGE

SPIRITUAL FREEDOM

Introduction

This book is not to decide how another person should live. My purpose is to let people know that change is possible if they are not happy or fulfilled in their current lifestyle. If you believe in Jesus and what the Bible says and you desire change in your life, you can be free. We all have to choose for ourselves how we live and the source we will be governed by. There is only Jesus and Satan, good and evil, right and wrong, heaven and hell. There is no middle ground or neutrality. Believing or not believing the truth doesn't make it any less true. You are born again or in sin.

God isn't willing that any should perish but have everlasting life through Jesus. (2 Peter 3:9 The Bible is the standard by which all men/women should live. It is always contrary to what the world approves of and condones. I sincerely pray my testimony plants seeds in your heart that will encourage you to step out in faith and walk in the obedience of God's written and spoken word. Know that you can sincerely turn your heart toward God when the Holy

Spirit draws you. Your struggle doesn't have to be perversion or anything deemed unrighteous by the word. This book's spiritual principles can be applied to any form of bondage you may be dealing with. There is hope in Jesus for every man, woman, boy, and girl. If you've tried everything and no results, now try Jesus.

SPIRITUAL
BONDAGE

Psalm 51:5
"Behold, I was shapen in iniquity; and in sin did my mother conceive me."

Chapter 1

The Seed

One day, in particular, stands out in my memories. I was five years old, and I had to stay home from school with my Dad. I had a terrible fever. My clothes were removed, except my underwear, to help my body cool down. As any kid would, I laid under him for comfort. This day would change my life forever. At some point, my Dad began to caress me. It was the first time I could recall having him to myself and spending quality time together.

It felt great to get undivided attention from him for once. He wasn't the emotional nor nurturing type of man. As I found comfort laying under him, it started to feel weird very quickly. He eventually got completely naked. He instructed me to lay on top of him. It was a very awkward feeling but comforting at the same time. This event was the beginning of him grooming me for inappropriate intimacy between the two of us. Time went on, and the fondling and caressing became more intense. It was tough to process as a young child what was taking place.

I grew up in Los Angeles, California, with both parents and one brother. Due to my Mom being a hard worker and great with finances, we lived a satisfying life. Our home was beautiful, and things seemed very normal for us from the outside looking in. My Mom was an elementary school teacher, faithful church worker, and choir member. My Dad rarely attended church. He was a steel mill worker and then became a bartender. I had one brother who was two years older, and we were very different. I had always wished for a sister to boss around, style her hair, and dress her up. I was fashionable and outgoing. My brother was the opposite, very laid back and plain in style, but he and my Dad shared a love for sports.

Dad and I had nothing in common outside of our weird secret encounters. I idolized my Mom. We went everywhere and did everything together. I would accompany her to the market, beauty salon, shopping, visiting friends, and church, of course. Growing up in school, I was slightly feminine because I had taken on my Mom's traits. I quickly learned that I had to defend myself and stand up to others because being different made some people uncomfortable.

I was raised in a traditional Baptist church and baptized in water around the age of ten. I have many great loving memories that happened there. We were like one big family.

I had many friends, and we had fun growing up together. At one point, I was the youngest member of the youth choir. I proudly sang soprano until the voice change happened. But to my surprise, I had to deal with some bullying even at church.

My Mom was in charge of programs for the kids; Easter, Christmas, and Thanksgiving services. One day, the church bully kept taunting me, and I blacked out. My friends said I beat the mess out of him. I just snapped. I was the type of person who could get along with anyone for the most part. I didn't really like confrontation, but something inside me would explode if you went too far. People had no idea what I was dealing with at home. I was a mini time bomb ticking. Needless to say, I got my respect at church, and nobody ever messed with me again, LOL. I felt terrible after the fight because my Mom had a huge influence over the kids and I felt pressured to be on my best behavior at all times. Fortunately, most people were aware of the bully's actions, and they thought he got what he deserved.

You may be wondering how things eventually progressed with my Dad and me after the initial experience. Well, my Mom worked pretty far away, which meant she got home later than I did. My brother arrived home later as well. My Dad being a bartender at night meant he was home during the day. I never wanted to be there with him alone. When I got out of school, I would try to stay outside until Mom came home, but sometimes it just didn't work out that way. He would demand me to come inside. It was the perfect setup in his favor. The fondling over time progressed to him pressuring me for oral and even anal service. Fortunately, I was always able to fight him off about the anal thing, so he never succeeded in that quest. Basically, oral sex was what it all boiled down to. The only consolation I had about the whole ordeal was that it usually didn't take very long for him to reach an orgasm.

The way he kept me in his grip was to tell me he would kick my butt if I ever told anyone and that nobody would ever believe me. It worked like a charm. Being that my first sexual experience was with him, it confused my identity. My Christian upbringing said it's wrong for men to be sexually intimate with each other. I went through most of my early school years trying to deny those feelings developed early on due to my exposure to sexual things.

In my teens, I began to be very promiscuous secretly. Even though I grew up Christian, in many churches, especially within music ministries, you have some men who are gay. Some are open about it, and some are closeted. I participated in many choirs as an outlet from my circumstances. I loved going to church, singing in the choir, and hearing the Word. But I wasn't living a righteous lifestyle. I eventually joined a well-known gospel recording choir against my Mom's wishes. She knew of the rumors that the leader was known for inappropriate relations with younger men. She knew that some choirs had a reputation for being full of gay men. Unfortunately, my experience was short-lived because the choir leader, who has a star on the Hollywood walk of fame, hit me.

I should've suspected something wasn't right. One evening after rehearsal, he randomly invited me to the movies. I was so impressed to be hanging out with the in-crowd. There were a few others who joined us. Instead of dropping me off at home afterward, we went to his place. I was so uncomfortable because we were in his bedroom. He had this big fancy house with expensive furniture. He made a move on me, and I declined. Telling him no was not an answer. His status impressed most people, but he grossed me out. I didn't care about any of that. He was not happy that I turned him down. Instead of taking me home, he intentionally took a long nap and finally took me when he was ready. I think it was his way of making me suffer. The rumors went around that I was the new boy toy. What an embarrassment. I didn't get in the choir for any funny business. He was very mean to me after this encounter. I eventually left the choir because I was very uncomfortable at that point.

I was constantly in a mental and spiritual battle of feeling like the lifestyle I was in was wrong and feeling like it's just who I was. The pressure of trying to fit in and be accepted led me to get a girlfriend. I dated two girls during my high school years. I was intimate with one of them. I desperately wanted the approval of my peers. The girlfriend I slept with pulled a fake pregnancy stunt on me. She tried to pressure me for money to get a pretend abortion. I don't remember how I found out what she was doing, but thankfully, I did. That situation left a bad taste in my mouth for females; I didn't trust them. I thought they were all scammers.

In school, I just wanted to fit in, to some degree. Academically, I was a smart kid and got good grades consistently. In my senior year, my grades started to decline due to high stress levels. My counselor pulled me into the office and asked a series of questions. Under pressure, I told her what was going on at home. She called the authorities, and I was whisked away by police in a New York minute. I was mortified and completely embarrassed. The kids at school saw me in the back of a police car. So, of course, when I got back to school, they wanted to know what happened. I honestly don't remember if I told them or not. Some things just become a blur when you've gone through so much trauma.

I had no choice but to finally tell my Mom. It was a tough

time for our entire family. Was I lying or telling the truth? My Dad denied any guilt whatsoever. I was temporarily placed in foster care with a sweet elderly Christian couple. When I returned home, I felt guilty as though I was breaking up our family. Eventually, I knew my Mom believed me. She did have to go through a painful process of acceptance to get there. A few years later, they got divorced. My father had a history of cheating with other women from the bar, so he already had plenty of strikes against him.

My Mom was a class act; a very kind and sweet Lady. She fussed about minor things, but she was harmless. Mom loved her kids. We grew up middle class, and I mostly got what I wanted. I remember, one day, we were shoe shopping. I wouldn't leave the store without a pair of platform shoes. She was totally against it. I cried and pitched a fit until she gave in. I had to wear those shoes until they couldn't be worn another day. Hahaha.

She was a cleaning fanatic. We often entertained relatives and church members. Our house was always immaculate. She kept the yard well-groomed, too. She had a thing about keeping the driveway spotless. My Mom was known as Mrs. Ruthie by everyone. They all knew that if their car leaked oil, they better park on the street or they were going to get scolded for sure by Mrs. Ruthie.

Now, as an adult, I appreciate growing up with my Mother's standards. To this day, I do not tolerate nastiness and clutter. My Mom also held to very traditional views. I rarely brought any male friends to the house. I knew she knew about my lifestyle, but I didn't flaunt it in her face out of respect. I know she loved me, but she was clear she disapproved of that choice.

Once I had a crush on my gym teacher. My Mom found a love letter I wrote to him in my jacket pocket. She was so mad she cursed the day I was born. Deep in my heart, I knew it was only a moment of anger and disappointment. As an adult, even when I moved out, I would come to visit, get in her bed, or sit under her and annoy her; she loved every minute of it. I was always a kid at heart around her. I did have a smart mouth at times, but she would remind me who's the boss. We avoided the gay talk for the most part. I had the utmost respect for my Mom.

In my youth, I was her shadow. I regularly went to her salon appointments. I was fascinated with hair. After I graduated from high school, I went to beauty college. I now have about forty years in the industry. I have experienced amazing things and met great people along the way. It has been a natural and perfect fit for me.

I have memories of screwing up a head or two initially and then eventually perfected my craft to do did videos, photo shoots, and I worked with a few celebrities. I'm known for really great haircuts—no regrets about any of it. I have had so many incredible clients and coworkers, too many to mention. They loved me for me, and my salon relationships were like an extended family. They knew some of my stories and saw all the phases I went through in my young adult and middle-aged years. I've worked all over L.A. County from Inglewood to Beverly Hills. When crack was big on the scene, we were the premier salon for girls with hustler boyfriends. There was never a dull moment.

When I had started to embrace adulthood, my parents finally divorced. My Dad moved out of state. My Mom seemed to be free after she let him go. Unfortunately, she never pursued another serious relationship, as far as I can recall. I desperately wanted her to find love again. At times, I wondered if she was dealing with loneliness. I believe she stayed in the marriage to set a good example for us, and she did her best to make it work.

Sometimes, children are more aware of what's going on than the parents realize. I knew the marriage was troubled many years before the divorce. It pained my heart to see her deal with my Dad. He was a liar, cheater, lazy, and disrespectful. No marriage has a chance if both parties aren't willing to do their part.

Looking back, I think my Dad didn't know how to love. Perhaps he never experienced it in his own life growing up. When people have been molested or abused, sometimes, but not always, they repeat that behavior. I believe that having same-sex encounters with my Dad, before I ever understood what was going on, shaped my identity immediately as a child. For most of my life, I was thoroughly convinced it was definitely my fault somehow.

When I would wrestle and play with other little boys, I could relate to our bodies closely touching and rubbing against each other because it was already a thing in my life. I was aware of body parts and sexual things sooner than I should've been. As a kid, I saw other boys as sexual objects because my mind was being set to believe it was normal to have same-sex relations. Wrestling was a gateway to reinforce the perverted mindset that was being instilled in me. Even when inappropriate sexual things happen, the truth is it feels good in the moment. Part of my torment was that although I felt like it was wrong, I did like the physical sensation and arousal from it. It is such a complicated thought process to handle as a kid.

We didn't have very many overnight visitors. Occasionally, my cousins would come over. We were close in age. It was fun to be a normal kid at times. I tried to suppress my soft side around them. I knew I had to be masculine to some degree to avoid being labeled.

The boys in the neighborhood were very rough and athletic. They would pump my brother up to be a daredevil. Thank God he never seriously got hurt. I just watched him in his antics. Occasionally, I would play with them, but basketball and football were not my favorite things. I was average when it came to track, though. Trying to keep up with the boys and have a masculine image in the neighborhood wasn't easy.

I remember having to fight the school bully one day. Fortunately, it didn't escalate into anything serious. I had to pretend I wasn't scared to prove a point. Interestingly enough, many gay men have a reputation for being able to fight. Maybe because, in my day, it wasn't very socially acceptable. So I would say it was in our best interest to know how to defend ourselves against someone homophobic and confrontational.

Chapter 2

Roots

In my early thirties, I partied and did my thing but still faithfully attended church. One day, my Mom sat me down and told me about her cancer diagnosis. The doctor told her she had six months to live. She had cancerous tumors in her stomach; the devastation is an understatement. She opted for in-home hospice care. One of the greatest moments I had with Mom was when I was ranting about all these plans I had for my future. She told me, "Son, I'm already proud of you." A mother's love is just indescribable.

We had an Aunt and Uncle that also helped us care for Mom while we went to work. Both of us were semi spoiled brats who didn't know how to deal with such a hard blow. She reassured us she was at peace. She transitioned as scheduled. She was so prepared that she had paid off the house and all the bills. She even left us a substantial inheritance. The money allotted to me became a band aid to cover my deep depression.

After her death, I became destructive and more

promiscuous than ever. I was searching for some form of relief. As a result of having a large amount of money at my access, I begin to shop regularly on Rodeo Drive in Beverly Hills. I've always been the fashion guy, but this was me on steroids. When my friends were in the area, they would come by the salon to see what my outfit of the day was. I got a kick out of it for sure. I felt like being known for my fashion sense was something to be proud of.

Whenever I would get down in the dumps, I would shop and sleep around. It was a never-ending path of bondage and destruction. The crazy thing is through all that I have encountered, I still pretty consistently attended church and stayed in music ministry. There was a point where I stopped attending for a season. I was just so hurt and angry with God. And I experienced some things at church that added to my disappointments.

The very environment that was supposed to bring me healing, hope, and deliverance was just another source of more hurt and pain at times. I've been a part of many Christian churches and fellowshipped with various people within the church community. Many of those relationships turned sour. I was manipulated and seduced by men, including those in ministry within my church affiliations. I would like to emphatically state that all churches and ministers do not condone nor behave in such ways as I've aforementioned. The encounters I had in some of my church experiences added to my pre-existing confusion and trauma. It caused me to wonder if deliverance was real or even possible. If you can't find solace and comfort in the church, then where?

Not seeing much of a representation of deliverance in the church caused me to believe it was an unrealistic goal. I became more comfortable and solidified in my double life. I felt like it's just the way things are. But In the back of my mind, I knew what the Word said about the lifestyle I was living, but what I was seeing Sunday after Sunday suggested something contrary.

My brother and I didn't talk much about personal matters, especially not things of a sexual nature. The only deep conversation we ever had was me asking him if Dad ever touched him inappropriately, and he said no. I honestly believe him because I saw absolutely no signs of anything otherwise.

Being submissive to my Dad, led me to be that same way with other men. I was attracted to masculine guys mostly. It included guys in the closet. Many of them were in denial about their sexuality. As a teen, I started drinking and smoking weed. Getting high was my thing. It was a gateway that allowed me to get in the right mood for the numerous sexual encounters. What surprised me is that masculinity doesn't automatically mean a man is straight.

At some point, even when I felt convicted about what I was doing, I had been doing it so long I didn't have the strength to resist my promiscuity. I tried drenching myself in continual church attendance. Occasionally, I could abstain from my desires temporarily, but it was never a real, lasting change. It had to start with repentance and a change of heart, and a mind reset. It's something that requires total surrender to God. You must come out of agreement with sin and agree with God's word.

I wasn't ready nor knowledgeable of the actual commitment that needed to be made for true change to take place. I thought that perhaps deliverance was a one-time trip to the altar where someone laid hands on you, and a prayer was spoken over you, and deliverance was instant. God can definitely move suddenly in a person's life, but that wasn't my experience. My deliverance was definitely a process.

I used gospel music in the same way I used sex and weed. It was all about a temporary escape. Anything that could make me feel good at the moment was appealing to me. The highlight of attending church was the singing and dancing. I did love hearing the Word of God as well, but not first and foremost as I should've. I lacked intimacy with God, which is essential to growing in him.

Attending church was an emotional high that I sought after. I would dance, cry, fall out, and even run around. I've always had a love for God but not in its fullness. God says in his Word if you love me, keep my commandments. (John 14:15) I learned how to look, act, and talk the part of being what we call 'churchy.' God calls it having a form of godliness but denying the power therein. (2 Timothy 3:5) I did not value nor strive to be like God in his holy character and nature. Like many people, I just wanted to feel good and know the God of tangible blessings. God is a multifaceted Spirit. He's more than just love and grace; he is a just God and a consuming fire.

I'm often asked why I don't drive. I'm a good driver with a heavy foot. I once owned a pale yellow '67 T Bird. It didn't last long because I knew nothing about older cars and had trouble finding mechanics for maintenance and repairs. I like public transportation because I can people watch and not have to deal with L.A. traffic or expensive gas prices. I've had some interesting experiences on the bus for sure.

One particular day, I was about to get off the bus at my stop. I just so happened to be going to church. An elderly lady began talking to me. She gave me specific instructions; she said, "Ask God to make me the man he called me to be and that I may fulfill my purpose in life for the glory of God."

Why would she say those things to me? She didn't

know me. I was in my early twenties when she told me those words. Her words have always stuck with me. It stopped me in my tracks momentarily. I knew it was a word from God, and many, many years later, I understood the full meaning of what she said. God was referring to my God-given spiritual identity versus who I thought I was in my flesh based on my actions. Identity is a huge factor in understanding Biblical truth and your position in Christ.

FIRST EXPERIENCES & STEPPED ON

I met a guy in the community choir I had joined in my late teens. He was my first adult gay friend, and I had many first experiences with him. We were platonic friends but were very close. He influenced me to smoke weed, drink and took me to my first gay club. He was a great singer and popular in the gay crowd and church scene. The problem was he was very two-faced. He would talk about me behind my back regularly. He did disrespectful things like leave me at the club to hook up with some random guy. I put up with it for many years. We had so many things in common, so I just dealt with all the mess in between.

Wanting to be accepted and loved so desperately caused me to be a doormat at times. I think the abuse desensitized me and toxic friendships seemed normal to some degree. My Dad had already betrayed me, so these types of friendships were not new to me. Looking back, I'm sure people wondered why I dealt with such a disrespectful friend. Hanging with him took me away from the drama at home. He showed and taught me a lot of things I never knew existed. I felt obligated to him in some weird way. Later in life, he was stricken with cancer of the throat and died. After he died, I was sure I wouldn't have any more crazy, one-sided, disrespectful friendships.

I thought I had enough with toxic relationships, but in time I knew I hadn't. A client of mine and I hit it off instantly and became very close. She was a go-getter, and that inspired me. She was always thinking and working on creative ways to make money. Yoyo had a side to her that was intense. She could be super nice or super mean, depending on the day. I dismissed it because that's just how she was. But I considered her to be family for sure. Remember when I said I always wanted a sister, she was that sister. Even though the relationship was toxic, I felt obligated and loyal to her because she was there for me during some rough times, like my Mom's passing. Yet, she still had a special place in my heart.

In her quest to always make money, I found out she had a connection to credit card fraud/identity theft. I never got involved in any of it, but we did go shopping together. I had my own money from my salon job and inheritance. In my state of depression, I went through most of my inheritance money. The majority of the time, we shopped at high-end department stores; Gucci, Neiman Marcus, etc. Knowing she used fake credit cards when she shopped, I would always feel slightly uncomfortable at the register, even though she was very smooth.

My brother and I weren't getting along living in our house together. He was doing his own thing with no regard for the house rules we had established. He had all types of shady people coming to our house. One day, my favorite shirt came up missing. It was a sparkly purple shirt that cost me $300. That was expensive in those days. I began to realize we couldn't live together. Shortly after that incident, I found out that he had forged my signature and took a loan out on our house. He was able to get out half the equity. When I learned about it, I sold it and got half of the home's value—wow, betrayed by my brother. Where does it end? I almost choked him out when the mortgage company called and told me what was going on. But the Holy Spirit told me to let him go. Shortly after, I realized I had experienced temporary insanity. It is a very real thing.

The Holy Spirit spoke to me, and my obedience kept me from going to prison for murder. It was an audible voice, and it was very soft and serene. I could have easily missed it, but God was so gracious to interrupt my plan. I didn't clearly understand the magnitude of that experience at the time. Glory to God! I did eventually forgive him. I love my brother.

I wasn't so great with managing finances. I asked Yoyo to put the money from the sale of the house into an account. I put it out of my mind as if it was money I didn't have. I was still doing well for myself while I was working at a salon in Beverly Hills. It was huge and had a diverse group of ethnicities on staff. One day, the salon mysteriously caught on fire (insurance scam).

I lost all my tools. I reached out to my sister/friend to pull my money from the account for supplies. She was never available. She continually gave me the runaround and had the nerve to give me attitude about trying to retrieve my own money. I knew something wasn't right. She had access to that money for several years. Come to find out, she had siphoned every dime I had and, of course, lied about it. I could've strangled her in seconds. She lied and said it was tied up in an investment with one of her shady friends. Why do the people I'm closest to seem to break my heart? Needless to say, that friendship ended.

I thought about pressing charges or even having her beat up. I honestly had to take some responsibility for it because I knew she had a sheisty side when money's involved. Yet, another costly lesson. God spared me again. Someone offered to take care of her for me, but as infuriated as I was, something in me declined the offer. At that point, I didn't have the money to pay for his services anyway.

Don't ignore the bad character you clearly see in people. I never thought she would betray me. I was just too trusting. After the falling out, I saw her one day in the church parking lot. I yelled out, telling everyone that she was a crook who stole my life savings. Believe it or not, I eventually forgave her but never dealt with her again. I heard she had a string of misfortunes happen to her after that. There was a fire in her garage, and all of my family heirlooms and pictures were destroyed. By then, I was accustomed to bad news. What hurt the most was disconnecting from her family. Her Mom, Dad, sisters, and her son were extended family to me. I couldn't deal with them and leave her alone. She was too evil and controlling to let that happen.

All of these heartbreaking experiences taught me to establish healthy boundaries with everyone and be realistic about who people are based on the character they display in their everyday lives. A desperation to be loved caused me to involve myself with people who didn't value nor respect me. You can and will be treated according to what you allow. In all of my betrayal experiences, I permitted people to continually abuse me because I put up with it in the name of friendship. If there isn't mutual respect and concern for one another, then there is no real friendship. I played a considerable part in my demise repeatedly.

Loving yourself is key. You shouldn't have to be abused in any way to have people around you. When a person doesn't value, respect, nor appreciate you, things will eventually go wrong, most certainly. For many years, I saw myself only as a victim. Insecurities, trust issues, anger, depression, rejection, and a need to be accepted and validated were things I had to get free from. But how? Going to church faithfully didn't automatically solve my issues. People would ask me why do I deal with those so-called friends. The truth is, I had low self-esteem and desperately wanted love and acceptance.

Chapter 3

Bondage

Always desiring the love and attention from my Dad and never having that void properly filled led me to continually look for love in all the wrong places. Weed was a big deal in my life. It gave me temporary relief, escape, and a sense of comfort. I was officially a weed head in my early 20's. I woke up smoking and continued day and night. It got so out of control that I even went to choir rehearsal and church services high on occasion. Lord forgive me. I was definitely convicted in my spirit for doing that when I decided to give my life to Jesus wholeheartedly.

I was also what you call a social drinker. Never an alcoholic, but I definitely had more than a few drunken nights. I remember falling out on the grass of a good friend after clubbing. I had to lay there for a short time to get my composure. It was hilarious. I've always been able to laugh at myself. Drinking, smoking, and being promiscuous sent me exploring the streets. I had my share of experiences in adult bookstores, theaters, and orgies. I've had encounters in public places like parks and even in a phone booth. We don't even have phone booths anymore, LOL.

One day, I stumbled on a place called the Pussycat Theatre. It was huge, and they played adult movies almost 24 hours a day. It was my Pandora's box. Although the movies were heterosexual, people there had all types of sexual appetites. They allowed sex out in the open. That place took me into the deepest part of my sex addiction. I noticed when I was bored or experiencing stress; I would end up in environments like that.

What surprised me was that I would run into guys on occasion from the church scene at all of those pickup spots. My ever-growing sexual appetite steered me into a very deep porn addiction. Even in my private time at home, I would spend hours viewing it. I would masturbate until it hurt to touch myself. I thought about it day and night and couldn't stop even when I tried to. I was totally consumed by it.

I had a thing for the rough, rugged type of guys. I can't tell you how many random guys were willing to hook up with me to get high and drink on my dime. Most of the time, they knew what I was all about from the beginning. Remember, I wasn't the typical macho type of guy. For some reason, I liked a challenge. I would go after the most masculine men, including thugs. It was as if I wanted the forbidden fruit, so to speak. I knew weed and alcohol were gateways to slip into sexual encounters. Many times, I entertained guys using those two things as bait. I occasionally tempted them with cash as well. I needed most of my money to keep buying my Gucci shoes. Lol

Once things got relaxed, the test was next. If they were comfortable watching porn with me, it was usually a green light from that point on. Many of these rough guys didn't identify as gay to themselves, so it was a hush-hush kind of thing if we got involved. It was like handle your business and get out. Many guys think that they aren't gay if they casually have same-sex relations but have no emotional attachment. And they don't go on dates. If you have lustful thoughts or engage in any sexual act with the same sex, it's perversion by Biblical standards. Let me give you a clear understanding of what perversion is. It's a twisting of truth or the misuse of anything outside of its original intent. It's not just sexual immorality.

People, in general, are inquisitive about certain things, including sexuality. I think it's possible for a person to have a same sex experience and conclude that it's not for them. Let's be totally honest. Sex feels good no matter who the partner is. The guys who do it secretly seem to view it as just another way to climax. Some of them are easily persuaded by money. Listen, if your sexuality can be easily bought with a few bucks, you would probably end up doing it anyway at some point. There was a song back in the day, "Blame it on the alcohol." Yeah right.

Inwardly, I longed for something more fulfilling. In the back of my mind, I always wondered if I was gay due to the molestation or was I just predestined to be that way. I knew most of my sexual encounters had no realistic chance of becoming anything more than what they were. But I tried to push myself on some of the guys anyway. I would attempt to wine and dine them as well as call them frequently. It never worked out. My desperation would turn them off, and they'd just eventually cut me off. Game over! Not being able to have steady, meaningful relationships just drove me deeper into promiscuity. A cheap thrill was better than no thrill, so I thought. At some point, I lost the desire for a serious relationship.

EMOTIONAL AND MENTAL BONDAGE

One of the most intense emotions I dealt with from childhood on up was fear. Being told something bad would happen to me if I told anyone was a nightmare continuously playing in my head. A few times, I wanted to drop hints to various people in my life about my nightmare; immediate neighbors who were extended family, church friends, and actual family members.

I couldn't find the strength to do it nor the words to say.

Thinking of my neighbor reminds me of how great a cook she was. Mrs. Ann could cook anything and put a southern twist to it. Occasionally, I was able to go to her house to escape the encounters. She had a son my age and foster kids. We would have church service downstairs in the family room or at my house. That's just what church kids do; sing, dance, playing the tambourine contest, and somebody would preach. Those were moments of just being a kid and having pure fun. A few times, I think we felt the presence of God.

Escaping reality was one of the ways I coped with all the inner turmoil. The pain associated with carrying such a deep dark secret was too much for a kid to bear. Many nights I cried and wondered, "Why me? What did I do to deserve this, God?" I learned at an early age how to hold things inside and put on a happy face for the crowd.

As I stated before, there was definitely confusion regarding my sexuality. All I knew, for the most part, was sex with men. I pretty much identified as gay. Sometimes, I was closeted about it, and other times I wasn't ashamed at all. I was fully aware that many people wanted nothing to do with gay people. Some people hated guys like me. I've encountered a few folks that name-called and heckled me but nothing of a serious nature. But I was not afraid to fight and defend myself if need be.

At home, it was very obvious that I had a chip on my shoulder in relation to my Dad. I avoided him most of the time. I always wondered if my mom just ignored it or did she have an inner knowing that something wasn't right. The few times I hung out with him, he would take my brother and me to the bar. I did like that because the owner was a very nice Asian lady. Mrs. Micky was her name. She always gave us unlimited Shirley Temples. Woo Hoo! The only other place we really went would be to one of his mistress's house. It infuriated me—just another reason to be angry with him.

He and my brother, on the other hand, got along great. I always wondered why I got picked for the molestation and not my brother. They talked about sports all the time, and that was the glue that stuck them together. Extreme stress was something I had no choice but to deal with. Knowing what was going on wasn't right but seeing no real way out of it was tough. What does a teenager do with that feeling?

My life was full of secret shame. This was my normal, and in some ways, I felt like the inappropriate attention from him was better than no attention at all—such a sad state of mind. The good thing for me was when I got to my late teens; I was physically able to resist him. I was old enough to go outside at will without his permission when Mom was late getting home. That's how things slowly tapered off for my good. Thank the Lord! Feeling like you have no way out of a situation creates a strong level of mental torment. Some people escape into a fantasy world or try to put it out of their minds. Other people are consumed by the terror and become introverts and paranoid in the worst way. Those are not things a child should have to endure.

FALSE

I thoroughly enjoyed growing up in the Baptist church. It gave me a foundation and Biblical principles to live by. I also learned about singing in the choir, my absolute favorite thing on earth. Being a very inquisitive person, at eighteen, led me to explore other Christian denominations. One day, at a gospel play, a warm sensation came over me suddenly, and without any thought, I began to speak in tongues for the first time. It was a mind-blowing experience. It was the beginning of me learning about gifts and manifestations of the Spirit. It felt as if God wrapped me in a blanket of His love. Actually, that's just what happened.

My next door neighbors were also Spirit-filled and a part of the Church of God in Christ (COGIC). My home church had lively services, but this other church was even more electrifying. They would dance very intensely, speak in tongues, had tambourines galore, plus a full band. The choir was all that. I was completely intrigued by it all. Sidenote, this church sold the best BBQ dinners. Everyone in Los Angeles literally knew it as the BBQ church. Ha!

Searching for something of a spiritual nature but not knowing exactly what led me to explore even more denominations. I eventually joined an Apostolic church where the pastor was very well known throughout that denomination. Following his passing, another very well-known leader took over, moved the church, and renamed it. I served faithfully in the music ministry for many years. Throughout my church history, I occasionally thought about what my life would be like if I got delivered from the way I was living.

One thing that kept me in a sort of comfort zone was knowing that in some of the churches I attended, there were guys who lived just like I did. I believe it gave me a false sense of security that I was okay just as I was. I never really saw what I would consider an authentic representation of what deliverance from that lifestyle looked like. The few men I knew, who claimed to be set free, would usually get busted for being with someone after their supposed deliverance. One of the reasons sexual immorality is an ongoing issue within many churches is because it stems from overlooking character and a lack of accountability even among leadership.

Church attendance can be a very charismatic and even soulish experience. Sometimes, people chase after an emotional high. There is a difference in emotions versus the Presence of God. When the Holy Spirit is at work, emotions are displayed because Holy Spirit can overwhelm you. But more importantly, there will be lasting fruit and change that takes place. All spiritual manifestations should ultimately lead you to repentance, wholeness, healing and point you to Jesus.

Many ministries focus on having people in positions who are gifted in a particular area. The problem is that these people will often get a pass to live any way they choose as long as the gift still works. The gifts are exalted above everything because the stirring up of people makes for a better offering. I'm not saying all churches are guilty of this, but definitely, more than should be. There are some key elements to a healthy ministry. The foundation of the Gospel is essential, along with biblical accuracy. When the uncompromised Gospel is preached, there should be miracles, signs, and wonders that follow. Healing, deliverance, the casting out of devils should be normal occurrences in a Spirit filled atmosphere.

The character of anyone ministering in the name of the Lord should display holiness and the Fruit of the Spirit. I have seen ministers of music who were great at it but were intentionally flamboyant about their alternative lifestyle, which should not be tolerated. As a result of seeing so much perversion in the church, I begin to think deliverance was just not a real thing. For some reason, I would still be convicted about my choices every now and then. Why was I feeling uneasy if it's my true identity?

I believe it's important for me to share with you this event of my eventual deliverance because so many people can relate to what I've experienced in the church and in the world as well. There's a part of salvation that is personal. You have to choose God's way or your way, and that will come with challenges and opposition. It will even contradict what the world-at-large and modern-day society believe and stand for. Walking with God/Jesus and developing a real relationship with Him is a very intimate experience. It's a matter of the heart and the mind. Glory to God!

Joshua 24:15 tells us we must choose whom we will serve. There are only two choices, God or Satan. We can't live to please God according to His word and simultaneously please ourselves by living however we choose. 2 Corinthians 5:17 says, "Therefore if any man be in Christ, he is a new creature: old things are passed away; behold, all things are become new." This is what's known as being born again, spiritually speaking. As my eyes began to be opened concerning a deeper understanding of God's word, the inner struggle and turmoil grew. I tried to convince myself I was okay, but deep inside, there was some level of conviction that I tried to brush off.

I continued being churchy on Sundays and doing me the rest of the time. This is what some people embrace is church membership, attendance, and a religious spirit. It's a double-minded and hypocritical position. You claim to love God and serve Him, but some of us live a life contrary to how the Bible admonishes a Believer to live. In scripture, it's referred to as having a form of godliness but denying the power therein. (2 Timothy 3:5) It's also referred to as being lukewarm. There's good news, though. The Holy Spirit can and will help you embrace a holy life versus living to please your flesh and follow after the things of the world. It's a choice that requires submission and obedience to the Word of God and His will, which ultimately is His word.

The truth is that many people only want God as a source of blessings or as a rescuer in times of trouble. The rest of the time, they want no accountability and want to do whatever pleases them. Let me tell you that there are some blessings that God will only give to those who are in covenant with Him. This means God honors those who live a holy life and obey His word. Salvation is full of benefits, much more than just going to Heaven. When I say living holy, I'm referring to living in obedience and submission to God's Word and denying of satisfying the flesh. It's loving what God loves and hating what God hates.

We don't hate any group of people. But as Believers, we have a guideline of how to live, know what we should support, and condone based on scriptures. Thankfully, I eventually heard a few testimonies of people who were set free, and there was no scandal or discrepancies surrounding them. I was introduced to a nationwide group of men who had all been set free from sexual immorality and were on fire for God. My prayer was answered. I now had hope for myself. We gathered regularly in our local groups and annually in the bigger group to pray, testify, study scripture, and encourage each other. What a blessing it was indeed. When I was in the men's group, I experienced a time of freedom from my addictions.

Chapter 4

Tree Branches

Being extremely promiscuous desensitized me from wanting serious relationships. I did, however, have a few of them. There was a nail salon next door to the hair salon, and I was getting a manicure. I noticed a guy staring at me. We engaged in conversation, and I knew he was interested. Come to find out; his sister was someone's client at the salon.. We began to get to know one another, and things progressed. He told me he was unhappily married. I fell for it and became sexually and emotionally involved. Typically. I preferred well-endowed men. He didn't measure up to that at all. Interestingly, enough I was madly in love with him.

Sex is physical, but he had my mind. I was more into him than most of the guys I've encountered. Emotional attachment is much more intoxicating than just a sexual thing. Soul ties can grip you and overtake your life. At some point, I realized he wasn't going to get a divorce and that I had been strung along. I also dealt with the guilt and shame of being involved with a married man.

One day, I got the strength to break it off. I vowed not to do the adultery thing moving forward. It was hard getting over him because I had believed we would eventually be together. I came to myself and began to think there is no future with a cheater. Sometimes, you don't want to accept what you know is true.

Many years later, I was coming out of a convenience store. My eyes locked with this thuggish handsome man, and we hit it off instantly. He, too, was a hairstylist, and we had lots of fun together. His outgoing and loving spirit captivated whomever he encountered. He and my best female friend hit it off as well, and he started working in her salon. Although he liked me, something was holding him back from fully committing. I thought maybe he was just a player.

Well, after some time, he moved into my place, and that's when the real story unfolded. He would occasionally disappear for days at a time. I assumed he was cheating. Come to find out; he was cheating. Her name was CRACK! In my desperation to prove to myself that I could have a successful relationship, I believed the lie that I could fix him by just loving him enough. I would try to make plans and occupy all of his free time to keep him from using.

One night, I went to the market to purchase ingredients to cook his favorite meal; fried chicken with soul food side dishes. When I came home, Mr. Man was gone for real. I hated the sight of fried chicken for months. Ha! He only got worse. I went to drag him out of his pretend cousin's house after they pulled an all-night session. In the midst of trying to control his life, I started to lose my own identity. My only concern was trying to fix him.

One night, I camped out at the salon. I was monitoring when he would be finished so he could come straight home with me. Another friend/coworker caught me peeking around the corner at the salon. I knew my mind was gone at that point. I was so embarrassed because I would typically talk bad about someone acting in this manner.

When Mr. Man moved to L.A., he had a preexisting history of substance abuse, and I was totally unaware of that. Unfortunately, he started to relapse around the time we met. I had let my mind go into the darkest depression ever. My best friend picked me up one day. She parked on the street. I had to cross an island to get to her. She told me I almost got hit by a car on each side of the island because I walked straight into traffic like a zombie. I never looked in either direction. That was my wake-up call to let him go back home, up north, so he could get the help he needed.

It was a valuable lesson for me not to ever love someone to the point of losing myself and neglecting my own well-being. You can't make someone love you, nor can you make choices for another adult. Praise God he was able to get control of his life and beat the addiction. His Mom was a minister. I believe she helped him get free. Thank you, Jesus!

Now, the very last serious relationship I had was also "complicated." We knew each other from the church scene and quickly became friends on social media. He was a sweet guy, no pun intended. Ha! He was a spoiled brat like myself. We hit it off and became serious. He was younger than I, and he liked to get out from time to time with his friends and family. I more so wanted to be a homebody and cuddle. We came to a happy medium and got through that part.

The twist to the plot is that he was an ordained/licensed minister. I often wondered how he navigated between the two lives. We didn't talk about it in-depth or hardly at all, for that matter. As things became serious, we contemplated moving out of state to somewhere that honored gay marriage at the time. It was only accepted in a few states. We wanted to adopt kids, get a dog, and have the whole white picket fence scenario. One of us could have used our sperm, but that could've been more drama, costly expenses, and legalities. This is where my deliverance started. Since we were making a life-changing move, I needed to be 100% sure that I was doing the right thing.

Wrestling internally with whether or not that life was okay with God caused me to search for a clear answer. I had a friend who was much more like a sister. She loved me unconditionally, but I knew she stood for holiness, and she lived it. I knew by her example that it was actually possible to live that way. I also had a friend at church who was faithful in intercessory prayer. I called her and told her my dilemma. She said, "You don't need my opinion or my judgment. You need to pray and ask God to speak directly to you and illuminate His word for you to see clearly."

I got on my knees and sincerely prayed for God to reveal the truth about His word and my identity in Him. The next day, I received all the answers I needed. First, God took me to Genesis 1:27 and showed me his original plan was specifically for a man and woman to be together. Then he took me to the book of Romans 1. It talks about the sexually immoral and that they will not enter Heaven. It even talked specifically about men being with men and women with women as something that God totally disapproves of. It goes against the very plan, nature, and character of God. I had my definite answer.

Well, now that I know what I should do, how do I get out of this mess I'm in? The first step was to break up with my friend and also tell all my close running buddies that

I no longer desired to exist in that life. This was a very overwhelming and scary time for me because I had no clue what was next. The changing of my mind happened overnight, and my partner was devastated. It didn't go well at all. I think he felt betrayed and dropped like a hot potato. I thought, by him being a minister, he would understand the spiritual aspect of my decision, but he wasn't having it. I think he may possibly resent me to this day. I pray that's not the case. All communication ceased between us. I heard that he eventually joined a so-called gay-affirming Pentecostal church. Imagine that. It's totally unscriptural.

Some of my running buddies or partners in crime were in the church, and some weren't. Again because this was an overnight decision, it blindsided everyone closely connected to me. I basically lost just about all my friends and had to embrace a wilderness process to lead to my healing and unforgiveness issues. This was my toughest battle ever, except for the trauma of losing my Mom. I had sincerely wished I had the one trip to the altar experience, and it would be all-over. But God didn't do it that way. Whew!

There were so many things that needed to be addressed for my freedom to manifest. Up until that point, I hadn't had very many demonic encounters or demonic manifestations in my life. Right after I made the change, I was demoniacally attacked in my mind. I was so severely tormented to the point that I got no rest nor peace. I had to pray in tongues continually for two days straight. If I let up, the tormenting would start immediately. Nobody told me that after being in gross darkness for so long that I'd be facing demonic backlash and retaliation for jumping ship, so to speak. Through this entire journey, God has been gracious to give me the tenacity to fight until the end. I had to deal with some pride issues and even some backsliding along the way. All of it has helped me to understand what true deliverance is and what it is not.

Now I have the tools to stay free by the power of the Holy Ghost. It is a divine ability available to all believers who fully trust and depend solely on Jesus! Oh, Hallelujah to the King of Kings and Lord of Lords! You can live free from the bondage of habitual, continual, and deliberate sin. People, in general, believe the lie that we can't help ourselves when it comes to sin. I beg to differ that sin is a choice. Did you know the word says with every temptation, God makes a way of escape? (1Corinthians 10:13)

Chapter 5

Brother

The Bible speaks of God as holy and righteous. Christians are to live by the standards set forth in the Word. We're to present our bodies as living sacrifices, holy, and acceptable unto Him. (Romans 12:1) The world's standards are the total opposite. In Christ, our lives are no longer our own. Our bodies are the temple of the Holy Ghost. Following the world's standards will pull you away from God. We're all born in sin and shaped in iniquity. (Psalm 51:5 Job 14.)

People can be born with all sorts of predispositions and proclivities; some even inherit passed down negative behaviors, or sometimes known as strongholds in the bloodline. Stinking thinking and dysfunctional behavior can definitely be recurring problems in families. These are false beliefs, false identities, even soul ties. I believe the early molestation was a strategic attack of Satan to sabotage my divine destiny in the Lord. There are many beliefs surrounding deliverance and whether or not someone's sexuality can be passed down. Most people know the popular saying, "once gay, always gay." Well, I'm a living witness that God can deliver us from anything that is contrary to His Word. This dispels the myth.

RIGHTEOUSNESS DENIED

Honestly, my journey to freedom was arduous. I thought it was going to be a fairly simple transition. How wrong was I? To my surprise, I even encountered opposition in the church. The subculture of gays I hung with saw me as a trader. Some people also labeled me as judgmental, self-righteous, holy roller, and a few other things. No one took me seriously. I wasn't mentally prepared to be viewed in such a seemingly negative light.

Along the way, God placed a variety of Believers in my pathway for guidance, comfort, and encouragement. I can't give one person credit for bringing me to the place I'm in now. It was a divine appointment. God, Jesus, and the Holy Spirit get all the credit for the victory in my life. It's sad that when true deliverance happened in my life, it was a taboo subject for some of those around me who claimed to be believers. They were so used to and comfortable with my old lifestyle of sin that they were uncomfortable with the righteousness of God that was forming in me. I must admit I did get into a bit of self-righteousness because I felt like I was living a pure life all of a sudden. I had to learn the hard way that only God was the source of my strength. It was nothing that I could take credit for nor be prideful about. Without God's help, we can't be free from any ungodly act. Our human strength will fail us.

THE PROCESS

I spent a period of time feeling like a fish out of water. I didn't fit in anywhere. The changes in my life started with repentance, a change of heart, and a mind to agree with the Word. I had to get past loneliness, horny nights, demonic attacks on my mind, forgiving myself, forgiving my Dad, and more. A huge part of it all was to get over what people thought of me. I have known a few people who embraced deliverance, but it was short-lived. They eventually went back to their former ways because they weren't fully committed to the uncomfortable and humbling process. A great key to deliverance from anything is to develop a love for God that's greater than the love for whatever the desire is that has you bound.

I knew I had to prepare myself to do this all alone if it came down to it. Fasting, praying, studying, communion, and meditating on the Word are essential practices that must be implemented regularly in the life of the Believer. These disciplines strengthen, guide, and keep your mind centered on the things of God rather than on worldly things or things that feed your fleshly desires. Patience is essential. Deliverance can be like peeling an onion. There are many layers, and as you submit to God, he can do a great work.

My mindset had to change as well. I knew I wasn't a girl physically, but I had taken on a feminine mindset. I had to agree with the Word and embrace the fact that God made me a man and I should think, act, look like, and accept my real identity, which is only found in Him. God instructed me to throw out any feminine-looking clothes. It wasn't just about a look, but it was to address the whole man and not just what's on the surface. I stopped smoking and clubbing—no more casual sex. I was somewhat lonely but well on my way to freedom. One of the last things for me to break free from was porn. I was no longer sleeping around but still entertaining things in my mind. I had to let go of it all.

TRUE FREEDOM THROUGH
PERSONAL DELIVERANCE

On this journey, I began to take pride in the fact that I had actually changed my life. That's the problem right there. I had to be humbled and learn I was powerless and could do nothing without the Holy Spirit's divine enabling. Trusting in myself for strength lead me into a holier than thou way of thinking. I had to learn my only hope was in relying on the Holy Spirit to strengthen me and the grace of God to keep me. I had an occasional moment of falling from time to time. It was either porn, masturbating, or a quick secret encounter with someone. There is no secret anything as far as God is concerned. He sees, knows, and hears all.

Finally, knowing that deliverance was real and tasting that freedom made it hard to bear that after all my progress I was making, I was suddenly back at square one. Guilt, condemnation, and shame rose each time. I kept falling because I developed a prideful attitude and took some of the credit for my freedom. I had the nerve to think I was spiritually superior—Ummm...no, sir. You weren't. I realized living right was a daily choice that had to be made, and the battle with my flesh is ongoing. Learning to fully depend on God to be my strength was the game-changer. My walk became consistent finally.

Another lesson I had to learn was realizing you've got to give God your all. Because a dibble and dabble on occasion mindset will keep those demonic doors open and eventually lead you to a backslidden state of being. I thought it was no big deal just to do a little something here and there. The Bible talks about counting up the cost to walk with God. (Luke 14:28-30) That's exactly what I had to do. When I realized it just wasn't worth it to lose my place in God for a temporary sexual fix, I looked at living holy in a more sacred way, and I stopped wavering in my walk. Glory to God! Lust is never satisfied, and it leaves you more empty after each encounter.

I also had to be honest about what things were triggers in my life. Certain people, places, and things were off limits because they were open doors to my past. I realized the majority of my day-to-day activities had to be shifted in the opposite direction. Thank the Lord. He never gave up on me. Every failure and learning lesson helped me in some way. I am now porn and masturbation free, celibate, on fire for Jesus, and living a holy and sanctified life. I had to be honest with myself and know that some places I couldn't go and some people I couldn't be around.

The power of God doesn't force you to do anything. We've been given free will. God will lead, guide, and strengthen you, but it's your choice to yield and obey Him or not. Hear me. DELIVERANCE IS A CHOICE. Jesus asked the woman at the well, "Will thou be made whole?" (John 4). This book isn't solely about perversion. These Biblical principles can be applied to any form of sin, bondage, and strongholds. Jesus shed his blood for our sins and gave us the Holy Spirit to guide, correct, empower, lead, teach, and comfort us. Once we repent of our sins and get baptized, we are new creatures in Christ. My definition for repentance is to change your mind about sin and agree with God by turning the opposite way.

Our sanctification is ongoing. We are set apart for the work of the Lord and for His glory. We learn and grow to love what God loves and hate what He hates. The worst thing to do is be a lukewarm Believer. God would prefer us to be on fire for Him or stay in the world and do our thing until we are sincerely ready to give our lives to Him. Salvation versus going to hell is a very serious thing. Eternity is forever, and repentance is something we can only do while we are alive on the earth. I'm in my 50's, and I honestly might not have kids or a wife this late in life. I wasted a lot of time doing things that didn't produce anything good. I know God can redeem the time, but I'm content where I am in life as of right now. I don't need to prove I'm delivered by creating or living up to an image. My salvation is the most crucial choice I could ever make.

If you need deliverance, money, fame, marriage, children, and nothing else can fix that. First things first, it is my desire to encourage everyone that to this day Jesus loves you. He wants to save, heal, deliver, bless, and use His people to snatch souls from hell and bring Him glory. If you're alive, it's never too late to come to Jesus and be changed and transformed willfully by the renewing of your mind. In this life, we search for money, fame, popularity, and power. The

Bible says, "What would it profit a man to gain the whole world and lose his soul? (Mark 8:36-38) To receive salvation is the most important choice of your life. It's only in the name of Yeshua, Jesus, whereby we can be saved. Hallelujah!

THE TREE OF FORGIVENESS

After I got a handle on the deliverance thing, there was still something lurking in me that desperately needed to be addressed. It was forgiveness. Throughout my life, I blamed myself for the abuse. Somehow, it was my fault what took place. At different times in my life, various people give me a word saying what happened in my childhood wasn't my fault. I came to understand in order to receive God's forgiveness for the life I lived. I had to include forgiving myself. This process was eye-opening and didn't stop there.

Being in the church, you hear about forgiveness often. The Bible says we must forgive to be forgiven. (Matthew 6:14) I always said I had forgiven my Dad, but it was just the right thing to say. What about deep within my heart? I realized I hadn't forgiven him truly because just the very thought of him was repulsive. I had minimal contact with him, and the conversations were very short. The Bible tells us to honor our father and mother. (Matthew 19:19) No matter what he has done, I am required to be respectful to the man who gave me life.

From time to time, the Holy Spirit would deal with me about calling him to tell him I forgave him. I put it off every time. Eventually, the nudging became very intense and unshakable. That day finally came. Keep in mind my Dad has never apologized nor fully admitted to the molestation to date. I was prepared not to get an acknowledgment or an apology. I called and told him that what he did messed me up but that I loved him and forgave him. You could sense him smiling through the phone. He was glad to hear it. Still no official apology. His response was, "Yeah, things got out of hand." That was the best attempt at an apology I was going to get.

I began to realize abused people sometimes abuse others, not always, but it happens. I wondered what happened to him in his upbringing. I felt compassion for him because I realized something in him was broken. When I got off the phone, I had an overwhelming need to throw up; some call it purging. I was so relieved. It literally felt like I lost fifty pounds. A huge burden was lifted off my shoulders, and I was healed on a much deeper level in my emotions.

It's often said that forgiveness is not just for the other person but also for your freedom. I held on to that unforgiveness from the age of five until my 40's. It's never too late to do the right thing. If you don't forgive, it will most likely turn into hatred, resentment, and bitterness. The stress of it all can also manifest in some type of sickness or ailment as well as trust and rejection issues. No unforgiveness is ever worth holding on to. God is love. He forgives us daily. All that I've battled and been through was to bring me to this moment. I'm very humbled and grateful to say I'm free from it all. I now have healthy and godly friendships. I'm free from sexual immorality. I love God more than anything. I have peace and unspeakable joy. I've forgiven my Dad, and I understand having healthy boundaries with people in my life.

I'm still in the beauty industry. Life is good. Only God gets the glory for it all. No matter how long you've struggled with addictions or anything that is not good-natured, God is here for you. There is nothing too hard for God if you only believe. When you come to the end of your human ability, that's when God can do His best work. He is a Spirit. He isn't limited by time, anything natural, or earthly limitations. Jesus loves you, and so do I. I respect people who may have a different view than myself. I believe everyone has a right to live their lives as they choose. The problem is that nowadays, if you choose not to agree with nor support same-sex relations, then you are discriminated against and falsely labeled. I only choose for myself how to live. I don't have to agree with someone else's choices. I do respect everyone.

Chapter 6

Emotional High

"Come in a dry devil and leave out a wet Devil." That phrase is very realistic in many churches. A hyped-up service full of inspiring music, emotionally charged atmospheres, and passionate preaching are the key ingredients to supposedly "having church." When emotions control you, there is a lack of self-control which is a Fruit of the Spirit. When the Spirit of God or Glory of God manifests, people can react in all sorts of ways. Emotions have a place in it all because God gave them to us, but they must be subject to us rather than leading and guiding us.

Some people mistake all emotional encounters as being touched by the Holy Ghost. When emotions subside and nothing changes afterward, it's a red flag. You might be sweaty and tired afterward, but that's about it. When there's an anointing, an authentic move of God, hearts will be led to salvation and repentance. Gifts of the Spirit will go forth, then deliverance will occur, and there will be growth and lasting change. You cannot encounter God's presence and remain the same. There will be evidence, or shall we say good fruit, that will come forth as a result.

Many people don't know the distinct difference between the two. Sometimes, the Presence of God may usher in a very quiet, still kind of atmosphere, no running and dancing. He may want to be reverenced in a posture of humility and surrender. Laying before Him in submission, repentance, and obedience is powerful. God is multifaceted and multidimensional. He can't be controlled, manipulated, nor boxed in.

UNGODLY SOUL TIES

Like minds are drawn to one another. People who may be in sin, lukewarm, or even on fire for God will gravitate towards others like themselves. While in church, I encountered many experiences and friendships with guys actively in perversion as I was. Being around all of that gave me a false sense of security because I felt like it was somewhat acceptable and normal. My friendships were important and genuine, but the common ground was rooted in ungodliness. This was the foundation for ungodly soul ties.

We didn't inspire nor encourage each other to live righteously. It was more like we adopted a double-life kind of attitude. We had a church face, and then we expressed our other side after the services were over. We didn't take salvation seriously because we had no accountability for how we lived—all the while knowing what the Bible says about it. Some call this mindset "playing church," or a form of godliness. We made an idol out of gospel music, singing, and dancing. It's all a byproduct of being seduced by a feeling or emotion. When I had a sudden change of heart, I had to immediately cut ties with all of those friends. I had to repent and sever my agreement to walking in darkness with the others.

AGREEMENT OF DARKNESS BROKEN

When you escape the clutches of Satan, he retaliates and will attempt to backlash in some way. Glory to God, we have been given power over all his power, and we aren't ignorant nor afraid of his plots and plans. We renounce our former ways and seal those open doors shut. We walk in the newness of life and in the Spirit. We are new creatures in God! I soon realized there is no such thing as neutral ground. You are either in agreement with darkness or not. It was devastating and painful to lose my dear friends. I knew I had to move on, but it was heart-wrenching. I felt so alone and misunderstood. Somehow deep inside, I knew it was an undeniable part of the process, and God gave me the strength to endure it.

It's been several years since all this took place. I still

love and miss my former friends. I pray they all experience freedom and a personal encounter with God like I did. It is a life-changing experience for sure. Let me encourage you. For every Believer, there may come a time when it must be about you and God only. If you have to give up some people, places, and things, it will all be worth it. Nothing and nobody can love and give you the peace that passes all understanding like the Lord can. (Philippians 4:7) He can't be substituted by anything in this world. Stay with God.

SPIRITUAL FREEDOM

Here are some scripture references related to salvation, sin, and deliverance.

Genesis 1:27 - 28

"So God created man in his own image, in the image of God created he him, male and female created he them. And God blessed them and God said unto them, Be fruitful and multiply and replenish the earth and subdue it and have dominion over the fish of the sea and over the fowl of the air and over every living thing moveth upon the earth."

Genesis 2:18

"And the Lord God said it is not good that the man should be alone; I will make a help meet for him."

1 Corinthians 11:9

"Neither was man created for woman, but woman for man."

Proverbs 18:22

"He who finds a wife finds a good thing and obtains favor from the Lord."

Romans 1:24 -27

"Wherefore God also gave them up to uncleanness through the lust of their own hearts to dishonor their own bodies between themselves. Who changed the truth of God into a lie and worshipped and served the creature more than the Creator who is blessed forever. Amen. For this cause God

gave them up unto vile affections: for even their women did change the natural use into that which is against nature.; And likewise also the men leaving that natural use of the woman, burned in their lust one toward another, men with men working that which is unseemly and received in themselves that recompense of their error which was meet."

1 Corinthians 6:9

"Know ye not that the unrighteous shall not inherit the kingdom of God. Be not deceived neither fornicators, nor idolaters, nor adulterers, nor effeminate, nor abusers of themselves with mankind."

Chapter 7

Undo the Damage

2 Corinthians 5:17-21

If Any Man be in Christ

Many people profess to be Christian. Lots of us join a church and get baptized, some at an early age. Being born again is much more than being a member of a church. It's a spiritual experience. Some Christians live in the same manner as unbelievers. They participate in all sorts of things that the Bible forbids for the saints. The Bible says, "Faith without works is dead." (James 2:14-26) This implies that we can't just believe in Jesus. Works do not save us, but they should be evident in our lives after our initial salvation experience. Salvation is only by grace through faith, trusting in the finished work of Jesus on the cross. However, as a result of that change in us, we then have to put some action behind the confession.

When our spiritual change is authentic, there will be evidence of it. The Fruit of the Spirit develops in the life of a Believer who is constantly working out their soul salvation through faith in the Word of God (Galatians 5:19-23). You can't encounter the authentic power of God and remain the same. Throughout the Bible, when people met Jesus, they were forever changed, healed, set free, etc. Unfortunately, some people are poor representatives of Christianity these days. We are the salt of the earth and the light in darkness. (Matthew 5:13-16) We are called to a higher standard and to be separated and live differently from the world.

Many times, unbelievers encounter Christians whose lives don't bear good fruit, and it paints a picture of a hypocrite. In the church, the same is true in some cases. These people spend the majority of their lives being faithful in church attendance and involvement, but their lives outside of the church don't reflect a holy lifestyle and a changed person. It is sometimes called a religious spirit, a legalistic mindset, and a routine of going through the motions usually occurs in this kind of individual. It's also referred to as 'lukewarm,' having one foot in the world and the other in the church.

Particularly in music ministry, there are many talented, gifted men (women too) who deal with sexual perversion. Some are gay, and others are bisexual. It's often overlooked and goes unaddressed because talent is sometimes esteemed over character and good fruit. The Bible is clear that sexual immorality is a sin, including but not limited to Same-Sex Attraction (SSA). Unbelievers see the contradiction in them professing one thing but living out another. It makes people in the world not take Christians seriously. We are called to be holy, for God is holy. (1 Peter 1:16-17) Even for myself, I didn't see many examples of former gay men truly living a holy life after coming to Christ. Salvation is a serious thing. There is only Heaven and Hell after death. We all must choose. (Matthew 6:24) How we live will determine our destiny after death.

We can live a life free from any strongholds and ungodly practices. The Holy Spirit can empower us to have victory over our flesh and a transformed/renewed mind in Christ. We are to love what God loves and hate what He hates. Sanctification can be a process over time that occurs where we are set apart for God. We are freed from the mindsets and ways of the world to display the character and nature of God. Our lives bring glory to God and bless other people. It is crucial to understand we aren't 'sinners saved by grace. We are new creatures in the Lord, and our minds and hearts have been transformed. We now have the power over all the power of the enemy, including bondage to sin.

People tend to see themselves according to the appetites and behaviors they exhibit. Everyone that comes to Christ is given a new identity in Him. Anything that is not reflective of the character and nature of God can be erased from your life by God's power. He desires us to be free from all demonic influence and strongholds. Some people say they are 'sinners saved by grace. The problem with that saying is you can't be saved and still identify as a sinner.

Being born again speaks of a new nature and identity in Christ. We are sons/daughters of the Most High God. We are no longer slaves to our former sinful nature. We're redeemed and washed in the precious blood of Jesus. Hallelujah! A life that has been truly transformed will bear good fruit. Your life is no longer your own, and your body is the temple of the Holy Ghost.

Chapter 8

Dangers Seen & Unseen

A trick of Satan's is to persuade you to do something sinful just one time. The goal is to get you trapped in your mind and develop warped thinking, which turns into a stronghold. We, as human beings, like to believe we are stronger than we are when it comes to resisting things. Each time we give in to sin, it becomes more difficult to deny it. In my promiscuity, my flesh was only temporarily satisfied, but it opened other doors. There were some things I would absolutely not do at the beginning of my promiscuity. Fast forward to the end of it; I had very few limits.

There are spiritual and natural laws. Spiritually speaking, when we open doors through unrepentant sin, it gives Satan legal rights to enter our lives and cause havoc. We must repent and renounce the former choices in prayer to close those doors. Many times, I've been driven by lust and placed myself in dangerous situations. The Lord kept me through it all. I have picked up guys and been robbed overnight. One time, I had a guy over, and it turned out he was on drugs. I couldn't get him to leave the next day. It was a nightmare.

During this time of my life, I thought of the temporary fun I wanted to have. I met an older gentleman and we had mutual friends. Weed was a common interest shared by most of the guys I'd pick up and connect with. We started getting high together. He eventually told me he'd never been with a guy but he thought about it. We proceeded to be intimate. The next time he came over he said he was going to fight me because I turned him gay. I thought surely this dude is joking. We smoked weed and even had sex. When he got ready to leave he attacked me. I was so shocked. We ended up in the parking lot. He chased me around the cars. I finally had enough and I grabbed him and he fell. He eventually went about his way. I've run into him a few times since then but we both just kept going. People can be in deep denial about things in their lives. It's easier for them to cope if they somehow don't have to own up to the reality of those things. They blame others to escape accountability. The fact was he liked it but couldn't accept it. I felt bad for him. He was cuckoo.

There was another time when I had gotten high with a guy, and we messed around. Later he tried to set me up. He came back to my place, but something in my spirit caused me to be on alert. He was planning on robbing me. He had someone hiding outside. When I saw him and opened the door, he tried to barge in. God gave me supernatural strength at that moment, and I pushed him back and locked the door. You would think I would've stopped picking up guys at that point, but I didn't. I was so lust-driven. I was willing to take chances for that temporary sexual gratification.

The thing about lust is that it's never satisfied. It feels good to the flesh, but afterward, your soul and spirit are in a deeper deficit because only God can bring us peace, fulfillment, and contentment. You can abuse yourself by continually choosing self-destructive behavior. At some point, it just becomes normal to you. It's a result of being desensitized to sin and a false sense of identity. You believe the lie that your behavior choices are inevitable because it's just who you are. Glory to God, our true identity is found in Christ Jesus.

I know many people who have been seriously injured, and some even lost their life by picking up the wrong guy. Some men are known as 'gay for pay'. This type of guy sees himself as straight but will engage in sex for money. Usually, there is no emotional attachment or any outside contact like going to movies, restaurants, etc. Some men are known as down low. They are usually in extreme denial. They actually are bisexual. The problem is that they, for whatever reason, don't want anyone to know they are that way. Most of the time it's a secret between them and their partner. They typically have wives or girlfriends. Pressure from family, society, and even from the church can push them to perpetuate an image.

I've met guys who slept with me regularly, but in their minds, they weren't gay because they lived a straight life outside of our secret encounters. It's really an identity issue. It's hard for some of these guys to accept what they like sexually. Even though from a worldly perspective, being gay is now celebrated and defended, it's still controversial in many people's eyes. Whether you like it or not, the Bible says it's not God's will to live that way. Everything that God endorses bears good fruit. Two men or two women can't naturally have a kid. If God approved of it, then he would've made it naturally possible for two men or women to procreate just like a man and woman. That's really not something that can be overlooked.

I want to give God a praise break right here! I could have been in worst situations when it came to promiscuity, partners, and drugs. For some reason, I have met lots of guys who did cocaine. I had so many opportunities to use as well. I have tried a primo, weed laced with cocaine. But by the grace of God, I knew it was something that would ruin my life due to the consequences of cocaine addiction. Mainly the abuse that I have seen others go through due to their partners being addicted to cocaine. I had enough sense to stick with weed. Thank you, Father.

It says a lot about what God approves of and disapproves of. Unfortunately, many people want to serve God their way. You can't cherry-pick the Bible and obey the parts you like. God tells us to be hot or cold. He despises the lukewarm. Once I met a guy who smelled the weed I was smoking as I walked down the street. He said he had the good stuff. It was awkward when we met up because when he came to buy, we sat in his car, and he kept adjusting his package. I thought, "That's weird." He was telling me how he was a devout Muslim, and he loved women, and on and on.

I got weed from him, and we smoked together here and there. One day he came over, and he just seemed preoccupied. He was talking all this macho stuff, and he was about to leave. All of a sudden, he says, "Come on before I change mind." I knew what he was saying, but I was shocked. Mr. Muslim was on the down-low. So, I was right about what I sensed when he was basically playing with himself previously in the car.

Perception is everything. There are lots of people who don't think of themselves as gay because they only have random encounters here and there. This can be a problem in heterosexual relationships because they don't disclose this to their partners. It's totally dishonest. When I thought or suspected a guy was on the low, who was dating any friend of mine. I would tell them my thoughts, and then they could make the decision for themselves. Deception is just not cool.

I have seen people so sexually bound that they craved extreme torture. There's something called "fisting." You put on a lubricated glove and literally penetrate the person, sometimes up past the wrist. I met a guy and didn't know that was his thing. I was literally heartbroken for him. I still can't believe I did that to him. Yuck. Sin will always take you out farther than you originally intended to go.

Taking cabs was a regular way of transportation for me. To give you an insight of how far sin had taken me, I had numerous encounters with the drivers. I did this in exchange for a quick buck. I was always so shocked, how easy it was to proposition some guys.

Chapter 9

Renewing of the Mind

Romans 12:2

"And be not conformed to this world but be ye transformed by the renewing of your mind that ye may prove what is that good and acceptable and perfect will of God."

Philippians 2:5

"Let this mind be in ou, which was also in Christ Jesus."

Proverbs 23:7

"For as he thinketh in his heart, so is he. Eat and drink, saith he to thee, but his heart is not with thee."

Proverbs 23:7

"As a man thinketh so is he ."

The Bible speaks of the renewing of the mind. Our thinking is so crucial to living a victorious life. This helps us understand we are free and victorious according to what God did for us by shedding His blood matters. We will then be confident that we are powerful and virtually unstoppable in whatever we set out to accomplish within the Word of God and according to His will. All of Heaven is backing us up when we are in covenant with God and obey His Word. We have power and authority in Jesus Name over sickness and all the power of the enemy. Lack and defeat are not burdens we have to bear. Healing, deliverance, and breakthroughs are normal occurrences in the lives of blood-washed, Spirit-filled believers.

RENEWING OF THE MIND

When we have lived in sin and been caught up with the things of the world and with satisfying our flesh, we then need a renewed mind. We must accept what the Word says about us and walk in that. We must not let our past define us. Dying to our own will and our flesh happens when we submit to the Holy Spirit, and we hide the Word of God in our hearts so we might not sin against God. We come into agreement with what the Word says. The conviction of the Holy Spirit led me to come into a place of alignment with the

Word. I also had to surrender to God's will versus my own.

ISSUES AND RENEWING

Jeremiah 17:9

"The heart is deceitful above all things and desperately wicked. Who can know it."

Luke 6:45

"A good man out-of the treasure of his heart bringeth forth that which is good; and an evil man out of the evil treasure in his heart bringeth forth that which is evil: for of the abundance of the heart his mouth speakers."

Proverbs 21:2

"All deeds are right in the sight of the doer, but the Lord weighs the heart."

Proverbs 4:23

"Keep your heart with all vigilance, for from it flow the springs of life."

Often, people say things like "only God can judge me" or "God knows my heart." He absolutely does. But it's us who don't know it. The Bible is the standard for the

Believer to live by. We sometimes make excuses to do and say whatever pleases us and our flesh. To walk with God requires us to deny the world and our own fleshly desires that don't line up with holiness and righteousness.

Psalm 119:11

"Thy word have I hid in my heart that I might not sin against thee."

It should be clear by now that according to scripture, what's in our hearts will determine what we do and say. Many people identify as Believers, but as we know, "faith without works is dead." We are held accountable to live lives that glorify God. Every born-again person will be an ex-something when they've been changed as a result of being born of the water and the Spirit. It's a spiritual encounter and phenomenon.

The divine enabling power of the Holy Ghost helps us to no longer be a slave to sinful desires and even lifestyles. It's a matter of our identity. Remember who you are in God. We have a new nature in Him. It's a process called sanctification where we are set apart from the beliefs and actions of the world to embrace being more Christ-like. It's so important to understand we are friends and the Sons of God. We are joint-heirs with God. We get the revelation of our identity in God through the Holy Spirit and God's word.

Chapter

Fathering & Bortherhood

Because I only had unhealthy sexual experiences with my dad, I didn't know how to see men as brothers, friends, or role models. I had a distorted view of men in my life. They were only sexual objects to me, even at a young age. When I did occasionally have a real friend, somehow, I always ended up being attracted to him. In my adult years, I was so clingy and needy in the intimate relationships I had with men, not realizing the real emotional deficit was due to a lack of proper love from my Dad.

Just as God is our Heavenly Father, our natural fathers are supposed to teach, guide, protect, and love us. Only having minimal interaction with my Dad outside of sexual things clouded my thinking. I wasn't into girls nor was I into sports. I didn't relate to most guys around me. My brother and I were opposites. He was into typical guy stuff like sports and video games. I was into whatever my Mom did. So I didn't have a bond with my Dad nor my brother.

I felt like nobody really understood me. Feeling like I didn't fit in drove me to find comfort in being promiscuous. A moment of pleasure was better than no pleasure at all, so I thought. When I did have male friends, I would typically develop a crush on them even if they weren't gay. I didn't know how to embrace brotherhood or a healthy male-to-male friendship without any inappropriate activity. So, I just gravitated towards a few gay friends and mostly female friends.

To be a balanced person, we need healthy male and female friends and role models. I always felt like I was missing something as a result of not having an ideal father son relationship. In my Christian life, I've discovered Sonship with God is so crucial. Knowing that God has a desire for me to have an intimate relationship with Him and He cares about everything that concerns me was life changing. My identity as a son gives me confidence and a sense of belonging.

The Bible refers to Believers as part of a royal priesthood. (1 Peter 2:9) My Heavenly Father is the King of Kings and the Lord of Lords. Knowing who I am helps me live accordingly. I am blessed and have the power of the Holy Spirit living in me. I no longer have a story of shame, defeat, and bondage. I walk in love, freedom, victory, and power. Knowing God as our Father is crucial to knowing our identity. He cares about everything concerning our lives.

Sometimes, the void of not having a father in the natural

can be supplemented by a father figure and mentors. I had a very close straight friend. People suspected us as being involved with one another. We got drunk one night and I tried to grab his private parts. He declined and I was so ashamed. Our friendship didn't miss a beat afterward but it was a wake-up call. I didn't value brotherhood in my life. I'm grateful that now I can look at men and engage with them as friends and brothers without any perverted expectations or motives. He whom the son sets free is free indeed. (John 8:36)

I have learned that looking upon anyone with lust or as a sexual object is to dishonor them. We should see everyone as a living soul and genuinely care about their well being. Coming to grips that my Dad probably didn't have it in him to give me proper love and guidance was the beginning of my healing. Experiencing a healthy relationship with your father is crucial to feeling loved, protected, and properly guided.

GOD FILLS THE DEFICIT

There's a deficit created when you aren't validated by your father. God exhibits those important characteristics as our spiritual Father. We have solace and love in Him. He can fill any void we may have experienced in the natural. He is a Father to the fatherless. Every molested person doesn't repeat the behavior. Every gay person is absolutely not attracted to children. I was once presented with an opportunity to take advantage of a child. When I began to replay all the damage my abuse had caused me, I cast down that very thought immediately and never contemplated anything of the sort. Glory to God I can be trusted.

I'm known as Uncle Kevin to so many extended nieces and nephews. You can be the one to break dysfunction and unhealthy behavior patterns in your family's bloodline. All of the things I missed out on in my dealings with my dad, I found them in God when I got the revelation of Sonship. He is a good Father in every way.

Chapter 11

Spiritual Fight

2 Corinthians 10:4-5

"For the weapons of our warfare are not carnal, but mighty through God to the pulling down of strong holds; Casting down imaginations, and every high thing that exalteth itself against the knowledge of God, and bringing into captivity every thought to the obedience of Christ;"

Daily we are in a spiritual battle. We are all born in sin and shaped in iniquity. Due to the fallen state of mankind, God sent His Son, Jesus, to die for our sin. His shed blood on the cross was the full payment for us. We are justified and redeemed back to God by this great sacrifice to receive eternal life with God. We can't be good enough to inherit eternal life. It is only ours by faith through grace in the finished work of Jesus.

A constant war or spiritual battle is going on in this life. Even if we are unaware, the battle still exists. Our flesh wants to please itself and do the things it shouldn't do. No good thing dwells in this flesh. Sometimes, even when we desire to do what's right, we find ourselves doing the opposite. The flesh naturally wants to rebel against the things of God. This is why we must be born again (spiritually) and be filled with the Holy Spirit to have power over our old sinful nature.

The Bible tells us that we wrestle not against flesh and blood but against principalities. (Ephesians 6:12-13) We are constantly conditioned and influenced by the things we see and hear daily. Television, social media, family, friends, relationships all play a part in how we see things and the choices we make. When we are ignorant of what is Biblically classified as right or wrong, we may have a mindset that says it's okay to do whatever makes you happy. It's important to know that what God calls sin and what the world says is permissible are always in contradiction. Sin is to participate in anything by word, thought, or deed that goes against scripture. Even if you lust for someone in your mind, it is counted as if you actually indulged. Satan is referred to as the Prince of the Air in this world. He tries to influence and pervert or misuse things that God created and ordained spiritually that it may manifest in the natural to please him.

Human Identity: I am not perversion. I can't stress how important it is to see yourself as God sees you.

SPIRITUAL IDENTITY

When we find ourselves routinely doing something, we tend to take it on as a part of our identity. For example, a person who drinks heavily might call himself an alcoholic, or a person who's promiscuous may say they're a whore. The things we do aren't necessarily our God given identity. It's often the opposite. If our identity is found in what we do, then changed behavior would suggest a new identity. People define their identity by the things they do but don't realize what has driven them to do it. These are spiritual attacks and attachments that have come to destroy our spiritual identities.

My spiritual identity was attacked early in my childhood because Satan wanted me to see myself in a perverted light rather than my God given image. I was always drawn to flashy and expensive things. Not being secure in my identity caused me to be obsessed with my outer appearance. I thought how I looked gave me worth. I concentrated on my wardrobe to the point of obsession. Spending money I didn't have to look the part at all times. It didn't amount to anything because I was empty on the inside.

In this world, people seek tangible things. Wealth and power don't fulfill your spiritual void created when you don't have Jesus as Lord and Savior. The recognition I received as being a fashionable guy only provided a little comfort. Rejection, confusion, molestation, trauma were things that distorted my view of self early on. Your mind is extremely impressionable at a young age. Your first experiences shape your thinking greatly. Seeing myself with a distorted view caused me to act out according to who I thought I was.

We must seek an intimate relationship with God and His spiritual blessings before anything else. Salivation and all things pertaining to life in Christ are a part of our inheritance as Son/Daughters in God. As I came into the knowledge of who I am and how God created me to be, I faced serious spiritual warfare. The spiritual attacks wanted to stop me and destroy my intimacy with God, the Father. Demons attacked me directly the moment I decided to wholeheartedly give my life to Jesus and give up the ungodly lifestyle.

My mind was tormented day and night by evil spirits. I kept hearing blasphemous thoughts. I knew they weren't my thoughts, but it was unbearable to hear what I heard. The enemy tried to cause me to fear and be burdened down, so I'd just go back to the familiar place. I refused. I prayed in tongues and fasted regularly.

YOUR SPIRITUAL WARFARE

Spiritual warfare includes fasting, prayer, communion,

reading the word, and staying away from triggers. I had to recognize triggers that could seduce or entice me to go back into my old lifestyle. It's dangerous to think you can get away with dibbling and dabbling in sin. (Galatians 5:16-26,1 Thessalonians 5:22-24) Establishing and maintaining spiritual discipline is necessary, but it's not to be rigid or always a set routine. Holy Spirit may lead you to change things up periodically.

PRAYER TIME & DELIVERANCE

Prayer is communication with God. Sometimes, I talk to Him, and sometimes I have to be still and quiet, so I can hear Him speak to me. It may come through inspiration from scripture, an impression, or even a song. Prayer is a spiritual discipline and a vital line of communication for every Believer. Prayer and fasting build your faith and helps you to discipline your flesh. It also gives you a more intense sensitivity to God's voice. These disciplines should be done periodically as the Spirit guides or lead one to do so.

You can set a specific time to pray daily to build discipline, but you can also pray without a rigid schedule. The point is to pray daily and read/meditate on the Word. When we talk about a person abstaining from something versus being delivered, there's a difference. Abstinence can be a result of what is called willpower. At any moment, a person can choose to return to their former habits no matter how long they've been abstaining. If the desire is still in their heart and they never dealt with what it is that drove them to pick up the habit, they almost always go back to it eventually.

Abstinence isn't a bad thing, but deliverance is a spiritual change of mind, heart, and action. Deliverance is when God supernaturally enables you to no longer do something that is sinful or detrimental to you and others. It's the act of being set free from any form of bondage. It's not achieved by human effort. Completely trust in God's power to take away the ungodly desire and steer you in the opposite direction. It can happen by the laying on of hands, prayer, fasting, or by receiving a divine revelation of your true identity in Christ. All of these blessings, which will change your heart and mindset. It's the Word of God that makes us New Creatures, as the Bible calls us.

When deliverance takes place, you can still be tempted by former things, but there is the power of God within you that strengthens you to say no to those temptations. It's the Spirit of God that gives us this kind of strength. The Bible declares in our fallen state; there is no good in us. (Romans 7) We even do the things we shouldn't do and neglect the things we should do. This is why we totally trust and depend on God to guide us in our daily walk with Him. In our weakness, His strength is made perfect. I had to learn the difference between my ability versus depending on the Holy Spirit for strength.

When you know that your life has changed only by God's grace, it humbles you and makes you compassionate toward others. There's nothing I could've done to deserve it. No man can boast about his spiritual growth because it's the Holy Spirit that gets the credit for it all. This is working out your own soul salvation. At one point, I thought my life had changed because I did the work in my natural strength. I was sadly mistaken. I fell right back into that lifestyle because I was so self-righteous and sure of myself.

God told me I wouldn't make it without His help. I began to understand the need for God to guide my life day in and day out more clearly. Besides the constant prayers of "Lord, please deliver me," I trusted in the Lord to reveal to me the shortcomings I still had. I totally trusted in the Lord to do it. Then I became self-centered and walked right into self-righteousness. I had to learn to give my power over to God for the process of deliverance to play out.

This spiritual battle taking place in the world is between good and evil. The problem now is that people who believe in a Christian Biblical standard who does not condone or support things that the world does are now being silenced. Religious freedom and freedom of speech are being taken if you don't agree with the agenda and ideologies of the current world system. Persecution, censoring, and retaliation come in the life of the Believer who stands for Biblical morals. The world doesn't know Jesus, and they want to do everything that opposes God and His word. This is why salvation is a very personal thing. You can only choose the way you live for yourself.

Chapter 12

Transformation

Romans 12:2

"...be ye transformed by the renewing of your mind..."

Proverbs 23:7

"For as he thinketh in his heart, so is he: Eat and drink, saith he to thee; but his heart is not with thee."

Transformation isn't always instant. The initial act of deciding to live God's way is only the first step. Your identity in Christ is not embraced when you haven't been born again. To be transformed, we have to know and agree with what the Word says about us. We can't agree with the Word if we don't know what it says. God had a plan, purpose, and destiny for you even before you were born. He knew everything that would transpire in your life. He specializes in using life's circumstances to teach us things and as an opportunity to show His love by keeping us in the midst of it all and making us better in the end.

If you knew your Father was a King, you would automatically think and act a certain way. Why? It's because you'd know your identity as a son or daughter of royalty. That's how it is in the Kingdom of God. We are called a royal priesthood and Joint heirs with Christ. He calls us friends. (John 15:15) But most of all, He is our Heavenly Father. He is the One who sustains, guides, protects, chastises us, but most of all, the One who loves us like no one else ever could. In our spiritual transformation, we become dead to our sinful nature and born into a newness of life, guided, and empowered to live a righteous life enabled by the Holy Spirit.

HIGHER AWARENESS

Many religions and spiritual practices point to a higher power. They do not all specifically refer to Jesus. All things spiritual are not equal. The Bible tells us that Jesus is the only way to salvation/eternal life. (John 14:6, Acts 4:12) We must have total faith and trust in Him, and His shed blood on the cross as the payment for our sin. It's not achieved by works. However, when we are truly born again, we will produce the Fruit of the Spirit in our lives over time. The Bible says you shall know them (Christians) by the fruit they bare and by the love they have for one another. The inward transformation will show itself outwardly in our daily lives.

Know who is valuable in your life. To some degree, a relationship with Jesus is a personal thing. In your relationship, you must be so dedicated to Him that if no one around you follows Him, you will remain faithful. It's wise and necessary to be a part of a local assembly of Spirit filled Believers. The Gifts of the Spirit should be embraced, and Biblical soundness is crucial. Ideally, the five fold offices should also be in order; apostles, prophets, evangelists, pastors, and teachers. (Ephesians 4:11) You gain strength, knowledge, accountability, impartation, and encouragement from being around like minded people who love God.

True spiritual intimacy with God brings about fleshly submission. We are made of flesh, but we have a soul and a spirit. Our soul includes our mind, will, and emotions. Our spirit becomes one with God when we're born again. Our flesh doesn't want to obey the things of God. This inner spiritual battle happens to everyone. We need to be filled with the Holy Spirit to subdue the flesh and be led by the Spirit. The Holy Spirit is a guide, comforter, teacher, friend, corrector, and He empowers us to move in the power of God. The power is released by the baptism/ infilling of the Holy Spirit. It grants access to the Gifts of the Spirit. They allow us to do supernatural works through God, including healing and miracles. The miracle working gifts of God are true and real, including deliverance.

In my transformation and transition, I've learned not to rush the process. The main thing I didn't want to do was to come out of homosexuality and get with a woman to prove my deliverance. I've seen so many guys get with women, even in marriage, but they were living a lie. Sexual sin applies to heterosexual and homosexual acts. I didn't want to jump out of bed with men to jump in bed with women. When you sincerely give your life to the Lord, you will definitely have to get free from what people think of your past, present, and future. Your aim is to walk in love, but first and foremost, it is to love God.

In loving God, we must obey His word. I chose to live a life of celibacy until marriage. It is Biblical because fornication is sin. A few men that I know married but didn't were not totally freed. Some of their marriages ended in divorce. The others remained married but continued sneaking around with men. No thanks.

A popular mindset for marriage is that two incomplete people come together to complete each other. Well, personally, I believe a person should be complete within themselves and within their identity in Christ first. Looking to be completed by another person is not wise, in my opinion. The two shall become one is more about being a team rather than placing your identity in someone else. Praise God for the beautiful institution of marriage.

Honestly, at my age, I'm at peace whether I get married or not. My most important relationship of all time is being intimate and in right standing with the Lord. Glory to God. I am still learning to see myself as the man God created me to be. My former life influenced certain mannerisms, ways of communicating, and even style choices. So, I have to stay vigilant and watchful. In my transition and transformation, I talk and even dress differently. I don't believe it is God's will for a man to look nor act effeminate, according to the Bible. I represent God on the earth. I embrace the attributes and characteristics of a godly man.

When it comes to finding a woman, I have also had to deal with unworthiness. Feeling like no woman would want to be with an ex-gay guy. And this made me apprehensive about pursuing them. Coming out of a lifestyle full of rejection, the last thing I wanted to do was experience that again. If I put myself out there, I know someone will give me a chance. But honestly, I've become accustomed to my single, celibate life. The beautiful thing is that I'm at peace. I'm not lonely nor sad. I rejoice that I can live a holy life and not be pressured to please anyone but the Lord. Truly I'm blessed.

FREEDOM FROM MAN

One thing that should be understood is that the Bible and the world's views will always clash. Jesus tells us we will either be friends with Him or the world. We can't serve two masters. (Joshua 24:15) This world is ruled by Satan. When you choose to follow God's way, it comes with persecution, hate, and being misunderstood. You have to be free from the opinions of men. You may even have times where you'll feel as if you're walking alone, but if you draw unto God, He will draw unto you. When you're in an intimate relationship and divine covenant with God, you'll have a peace that passes all understanding. The joy of the Lord will be your strength to endure hardships and adversity. Be not weary in well doing for in due season you shall reap if you faint not. (Galatians 6:9-10)

Moving forward, I don't allow anyone to put me in a box. I have nothing to prove. My deliverance speaks for itself by the life I live. Some people think that marriage is deliverance after coming out of a homosexual lifestyle. If you get married but don't truly receive deliverance from your issues first, you're only adding to the problem.

I believe that's why many people aren't successful in staying free. It doesn't work like that. For example, if you struggle with lust, getting married isn't going to automatically free you from the spirit of lust. You have to deal with first things first. People are so concerned with image that they do whatever they need to do to be viewed a certain way. What we must remember is that God knows our hearts and our motives. We can't fool Him.

I have become comfortable in my single status. I'm honestly not sure about having a wife and kids at this age. Praise God I'm healthy and in my 50's. I'm actually content at this point of my life. I rejoice because God has given me peace in my current state. What a blessing it is. I'm free from perversion, masturbation, pornography, weed, and alcohol. Only God could've done this. Jesus loves you. He died that you could be free and have eternal life with Him. Today can be your day. It doesn't matter what your struggle is. It doesn't matter what false identity you may have embraced. Jesus bled, died, and rose again to save, heal, and deliver. You can be redeemed back into right standing with God. At death, every person will go to Heaven or Hell. You can choose while you're still alive. There's no repentance after death.

JESUS LOVES YOU, AND SO DO I

Chapter 13

Blessings in Freedom

Freedom is being able to make your own choices and the lack of restraints or restrictions. What may appear to be freedom can ultimately lead to bondage. For example, you are free to drink alcohol, but doing so in excess can turn that freedom into bondage. We are either governed by the Word of God and His Spirit or by Satan. You can be a good person and not have Jesus as Lord and Savior. Our sins must be blotted out to be in the right standing with God, who is Holy. Only the blood of Jesus can qualify as the payment for sin.

Real freedom is to no longer be controlled by fleshly desires, emotions, nor the ideologies of this world. Being Spirit filled and Spirit lead makes all the difference in how your life is lived. You can glorify self or glorify God. He does not share His glory. (Joshua 24:19, Isaiah 42:8) I can't tell you how grateful I am to really be free. I'm no longer tormented in my mind. I have forgiven my Dad and myself. Sometimes people live lives stuck in the past. There's nothing that Jesus can't heal in your life. Physical illness, trauma, mental issues, addictions, even New Age, and occultism are no match for the Name Jesus. He has all power in Heaven and in the Earth. Do not let the popular opinion of man deceive you. God's way is the only way. (Proverbs 14:12)

There's a way which seems right to man, but the end thereof is death. (Matthew 7:13) "Enter in at the straight gate, for wide is the gate and broad the way that leads to destruction and many there be which go in there. Because straight is the gate and narrow is the way that leads to life and few there be that find it." What the world calls a good life will mean nothing if your soul is lost. (Mark 8:36)

Walking in the newness of life by being in an intimate relationship with the Lord is as free as it gets. I'm a hearer and doer of the Word. I'm a son of God. My strength, hope, trust, and faith are in God. In Him, I live, move, and have my being. (Acts 17:28) No matter what you've battled with or negative things you can't seem to escape, know that Jesus is the answer. If I have been made free and whole, you can be too. The world says do whatever makes you feel good, but God says we must take up our cross and deny ourselves to follow Him. (Matthew 16:23-25)

When the word 'blessing' is mentioned, most people tend to think of material things. There is no lack in Heaven;

an opulent place. Our lives should be filled with Heavenly spiritual blessings. These blessings and prosperity have their rightful place in our lives. However, it's the priceless things that money can't buy that are of most importance; our salvation. It's only in Jesus that we receive all spiritual blessings. We are wrapped into Christ, and God sees us as His Sons and Daughters. (Ephesians 1:3)

He is the King of Kings and Lord of Lords. (Revelation 17:14, 1Timothy 6:15) Abba (Father) God, which is our Father, will withhold no good thing from those that walk upright before him. (Psalm 84:11) Receiving salvation isn't just about living in eternity with Jesus. We have been blessed to carry God's Spirit and His glory in us. We bring the atmosphere of Heaven into the Earth. No other God can save, heal, restore, and deliver. Jesus is the only way, and the only way is Jesus.

We only come to God by the drawing of the Holy Spirit. God speaks to us in so many ways. Most people aren't aware when it's Him because they aren't familiar with how He speaks. It's through His word, other people, situations, circumstances, dreams, visions, internally, and even audibly. Once, I was walking outside on a beautiful clear day. Literally, out of nowhere, I heard a strong voice say, "It's time to leave your church." I looked around, but nobody was on the street except me. I said I must be hearing things. The voice repeated it. I knew without a shadow of a doubt that it was God's voice. When this happens, it is something you'll never forget. This was shortly after I had begun my deliverance process. Needless to say, I left the church after that encounter.

As I stated before, a part of my freedom was choosing to forgive my Dad no matter how he responded. I found out in my youth that I had a sister from him. We occasionally keep in touch. I also found out there were supposed allegations about him inappropriately doing something with a minor. I couldn't take any more. I chose not to even get involved. The bottom line is I had to forgive him and pray for him.

I don't think a person will be set free from anything they don't want to confront and be remorseful for. He calls me from time to time. Honestly, depending on how I felt at that moment, I may or may not briefly chat with him. I'm okay with us not being close. That doesn't excuse me from having animosity toward him or showing any disrespect. I don't think I have the capacity to be best friends with him. But at the very least, I should see him as God sees him. He is still a redeemable soul.

At the end of the day, giving our lives to Jesus is the only way to have eternal peace. I pray something has been said to encourage you and to prick your heart. May the Holy Spirit have a divine encounter with you, and may you experience deliverance/freedom in your own life. Jesus loves you, and so do I. Repent of your sins and put your trust in the finished work of Jesus. Find a local Spirit filled church and get baptized in water & the Spirit. You don't know freedom until God has set you free. I'm here to dispel the myth 'once gay, always gay' is a complete lie. God bless you. Choose Jesus while you still have breath in your body. You'll either spend eternity with Jesus or Satan. There's no other options. Give the Lord a try. He won't fail you.

NOTES

Song

Fox. J. "Blame It." Jamie Fox. Intuition. J. 2008.